# Surviving the Night Shift:

## A Nurse's Guide to Work-Life Balance

M.A. Gorre

# Contents

# Introduction

In the dim glow of the hospital lights, where the clock hands creep sluggishly through the small hours of the night, the night shift nurses serve as vigilant guardians of health and well-being. I know this nocturnal world intimately, having been a nurse for almost 15 years. It's a realm oscillating between long stretches of eerie quiet and sudden surges of high-stakes emergencies, all while the rest of the world slumbers in ignorance. While the challenges of night shifts in nursing are undeniable—from the jarring disruption to one's circadian rhythm to the emotional toll of caring for critically ill patients when your body screams for rest—unique rewards make the experience worthwhile.

Yet, the imperative for a sustainable work-life balance remains even as we find purpose and satisfaction in our nighttime roles. This equilibrium is not a luxury; it's necessary to maintain the quality of patient care and our mental, emotional, and physical well-being. Neglecting this balance isn't an option when lives, including our own, are at stake.

In this guide, we'll delve into the labyrinthine challenges of the night shift and explore pragmatic solutions for harmonizing our professional responsibilities with our personal lives. Because when the night is darkest, we, as nurses, shine the brightest. Yet, that light can only be sustained if we also take the time to recharge and illuminate our own lives. Welcome to "Surviving the Night Shift: A Nurse's Guide to Work-Life Balance."

# The Science of Sleep

## Circadian Rhythms and the Night Shift Paradox

Sleep isn't merely a passive state of unconsciousness that we slip into at the end of each day; it's an intricate biological process that plays a pivotal role in our overall health and well-being. Sleep is regulated by an internal body clock, also known as the circadian rhythm, which operates on roughly a 24-hour cycle. This internal clock is influenced by external cues like light and temperature, helping us align our sleep-wake cycle with the day-night pattern of our environment.

## The Biology of Sleep

Sleep can be divided into two primary types: REM (Rapid Eye Movement) and non-REM sleep. Non-REM sleep itself has three stages, each progressively deeper and more vital. Stage 1 is light sleep, where you can be easily awakened. Stage 2 involves decreased muscle activity and reduced awareness of the environment. Stage 3, or deep sleep, is where the most vital processes occur, including tissue repair and memory consolidation.

On the other hand, REM sleep is the stage associated with vivid dreams and, paradoxically, heightened brain activity. This stage is crucial for emotional processing and memory. An average adult will cycle through these stages multiple times at night, with each complete cycle lasting about 90 minutes.

## Circadian Rhythms: The Internal Clock

Our circadian rhythm is regulated by a cluster of cells in the hypothalamus, the suprachiasmatic nucleus (SCN). The SCN takes signals from the eyes—particularly the exposure to natural light—and uses these cues to synchronize various biological processes, like hormone secretion, metabolism, and our sleep-wake cycle. Under normal conditions, our body begins to release melatonin, the sleep hormone, as it gets dark, reaching peak levels in the middle of the night and gradually decreasing as dawn approaches.

## Night Shifts and Sleep Disruption

For those working night shifts, this biological setup poses a significant problem. Night-time work demands high alertness and cognitive performance precisely when the circadian rhythm pushes the body toward sleep. This misalignment makes it challenging to remain awake and alert and puts stress on bodily systems, increasing the risk for a range of health issues like cardiovascular disease, gastrointestinal problems, and even certain types of cancer.

Moreover, night shift workers often find it challenging to get quality sleep during daylight hours. Reduced exposure to natural light can decrease serotonin levels, affecting mood and overall well-being. Besides, societal norms and daytime responsibilities, such as family and errands, can further fragment sleep, diminishing its quality and restorative capabilities.

## Coping Mechanisms

While the challenges are substantial, they're not insurmountable. Strategies such as timed exposure to bright light during work hours, blackout curtains for daytime sleep, and carefully managed caffeine intake can help night-shift workers adjust their internal clocks to a nocturnal lifestyle, albeit partially. However, achieving a perfect alignment is often difficult, making work-life balance even more critical for those traversing the nighttime landscape.

In summary, understanding the science of sleep and circadian rhythms is not merely academic for night shift workers; it's a vital component of maintaining health, optimizing performance, and achieving a sustainable work-life balance. Armed with this knowledge, we can better navigate the complexities of our biological clocks, making informed decisions that benefit our professional commitments and personal well-being.

# Physical Health Tips for Night Shift Workers

Working the night shift can significantly affect your physical health, but understanding how to adapt your lifestyle can make a world of difference. Here, we delve into critical aspects such as dietary guidelines, exercise routines, and other physical health recommendations designed explicitly for those braving the night shift.

## Dietary Guidelines

1. **Plan Your Meals**: Aim to eat regular meals spaced throughout your "day," even if your day starts when everyone else's ends. Consistent meal timing helps stabilize your metabolism.

2. **Balanced Nutrition**: Opt for a balanced diet rich in fruits, vegetables, lean protein, and whole grains. Avoid sugary snacks and fast food as they can cause a sudden spike and subsequent drop in energy levels.

3. **Hydration**: Keep hydrated with water or herbal teas. Avoid sugary drinks and limit caffeine intake, especially towards the end of your shift, to ensure it doesn't affect your sleep later.

4. **Smart Snacking**: If you need a snack, go for nuts, fruits, or yogurt. Avoid snacks high in sugar or fat, leading to weight gain and increased fatigue.

5. **Meal Timing**: Avoid eating large meals close to bedtime, as lying down with a full stomach can disrupt sleep and cause digestive issues.

## Exercise Routines

1. **Consistency is Key**: Establish a consistent exercise routine, aiming for at least 150 minutes of moderate aerobic or 75 minutes of vigorous activity each week, along with strength training.

2. **Timing Matters**: Ideally, exercise before your shift to boost energy levels or right after to help wind down. Avoid strenuous exercises close to your sleep time, as they can be stimulating.

3. **Quick Workouts**: If a long workout isn't feasible, short bursts of physical activity, like a 10-minute walk or a quick

set of push-ups, can also be effective.

4. **Flexibility and Relaxation**: Incorporate stretching and relaxation techniques like deep breathing or meditation into your routine. This can be particularly beneficial during breaks to relieve stress and improve focus.

## Other Physical Health Recommendations

1. **Quality Sleep**: Invest in blackout curtains and noise-cancelling headphones to create a sleep-friendly environment during the day.

2. **Vitamin D**: Given the limited exposure to natural daylight, consider taking a Vitamin D supplement after consulting with a healthcare provider.

3. **Regular Check-ups**: Schedule regular medical check-ups to monitor your blood pressure, blood sugar levels, and other essential parameters. The altered sleep-wake cycle can affect various bodily functions, making regular screenings vital.

4. **Foot Care**: Nurses are often on their feet for extended periods. Wear comfortable, supportive footwear and take moments to sit down whenever possible.

5. **Hand Hygiene**: Given that you're in a healthcare environment, frequent handwashing is necessary, but it can dry out your skin. Keep a non-scented, healthcare-approved moisturizer to keep your hands from getting chapped or irritated.

6. **Mental Health**: Don't neglect your mental well-being while

focusing on physical health. Stress-relieving techniques like deep breathing, short meditation, or even speaking to a counsellor can be beneficial.

Being proactive about your health while working night shifts is not just a personal necessity; it's a professional responsibility. When you're well taken care of, you're better equipped to provide the best care to your patients. Implementing these guidelines can go a long way in helping you maintain a balanced, healthy lifestyle, regardless of your working hours.

# Mental Well-Being

## Navigating Stress and Emotional Balance on the Night Shift

Working night shifts in a high-stakes environment like healthcare can be particularly taxing on your mental well-being. The isolation, erratic sleep schedules, and the emotional demands of the job can take a toll on even the most resilient individuals. However, the good news is that there are actionable strategies for managing stress and maintaining emotional balance, even when your schedule runs counter to the rest of the world.

## Mindfulness and Meditation

1. **Mindfulness Techniques**: Simple mindfulness exercises can help you become aware of your thoughts and feelings. Take a few minutes during your break to focus on your breathing and ground yourself in the present moment.
2. **Meditation**: Apps like Headspace or Calm offer guided meditation sessions that can be done in as little as 5 minutes. These quick sessions can help reduce stress and improve your focus.

### Communication and Support

1. **Stay Connected**: Although you're working when most people are off the clock, make time to connect with family and friends. A quick call or video chat can do wonders for your emotional well-being.
2. **Professional Support**: Seek out support groups or counseling services that accommodate night shift schedules. Sometimes talking through your challenges with a trained professional can provide invaluable perspective.

# Time Management

## Achieving Work-Life Balance on the Night Shift

Managing your time effectively on the night shift can often feel like juggling flaming torches while walking on a tightrope. Yet, striking the right balance between work responsibilities and personal life is crucial for maintaining both your professional performance and your well-being. Here are some tips and tools to help you manage your time adeptly.

## Planning and Prioritizing

1. **Weekly Planners**: Use a weekly planner to allocate specific time blocks for work, rest, and leisure. The visual layout can help you gain a clearer sense of your commitments and free time.

2. **To-Do Lists**: Create daily or weekly to-do lists and prioritize

tasks. Whether it's patient reports that need to be filed or grocery shopping that needs to be done, jot it down.

3. **ABC Priority Method**: Label tasks A, B, or C depending on their urgency and importance. Focus on 'A' tasks first, followed by 'B' and 'C'.

## Work Strategies

1. **Batch Processing**: Group similar tasks together and complete them in one go. For example, if you have multiple patients to check on, try to do it in one round to save time and energy.

2. **Time Audits**: Periodically, record how you spend your time at work. This can be an eye-opening exercise and can help you eliminate or delegate tasks that are not essential.

3. **Breaks and Rest**: Don't skip on breaks; they're essential for maintaining high levels of productivity and focus. A 10-minute walk or even a quick power nap can be incredibly refreshing.

## Personal Time

1. **Quality over Quantity**: Due to the erratic nature of night shift work, you may have limited time for personal activities. Make those moments count. Quality time, even if brief, can be deeply fulfilling.

2. **Personal Projects**: If you have hobbies or projects that you're passionate about, schedule time for them just like you would for any other important appointment.

3. **Family and Friends**: Coordinate with loved ones to find mutually convenient times to catch up. Maintain a shared calendar if needed to streamline plans.

## Tools and Apps

1. **Digital Calendars**: Apps like Google Calendar can help you keep track of your schedule and set reminders for important tasks or appointments.

2. **Time Management Apps**: Consider using apps like Toggl or RescueTime to track how you spend your time. These apps can provide insights into your work habits and help you become more efficient.

3. **Alarm Clocks and Timers**: Use alarms to remind you when it's time to switch tasks or take a break. The Pomodoro Technique, which involves working in bursts of 25 minutes and then taking a 5-minute break, can be useful for maintaining focus.

## Flexibility

1. **Adapt and Revisit**: Your priorities may change, and unexpected responsibilities may come up. Be prepared to adapt your plans and revisit your to-do lists and priorities accord-

ingly.

2. **Buffer Time**: Always build some 'buffer time' into your schedule to account for unforeseen delays and tasks. This can help reduce stress and make your schedule more manageable.

Effective time management isn't just about squeezing more activities into your day; it's about creating a harmonious balance between your professional responsibilities and personal life. By incorporating these tips and tools into your routine, you're not just surviving the night shift; you're thriving in it.

# Family and Social Life

## Nurturing Relationships on the Night Shift

Juggling a night shift job and maintaining a vibrant family and social life is no easy feat. While working unconventional hours poses challenges to social interactions and family commitments, it's not an insurmountable obstacle. Here are some strategies to help you maintain healthy relationships and an active social life while working the night shift.

## Communication is Key

1. **Open Dialogue**: It's crucial to have open, honest conversations with your family and friends about your work schedule, its challenges, and how it impacts your availability. Ensure

they understand your constraints and desire to maintain the relationship.

2. **Scheduled Check-ins**: Whether it's a quick morning call to a loved one or a weekly video chat with your social circle, ensure regular check-ins to stay updated and maintain emotional closeness.

## Planning and Prioritizing

1. **Shared Calendars**: Utilize digital shared calendars with your family members to schedule activities, appointments, or quiet times. This helps everyone be on the same page and plan better.

2. **Special Occasions**: Plan for birthdays, anniversaries, and other significant events well in advance. Request time off or swap shifts to ensure you can be present on important days.

3. **Prioritize**: While you might not be able to attend every social gathering or family event, make a point to be present for the ones that matter most to you and your loved ones.

## Make the Most of Your Time Off

1. **Quality Over Quantity**: Your time off might be limited, so focus on the quality of interactions rather than the number of activities you can cram into your free hours.

2. **Mini Celebrations**: Sometimes, working the night shift

means you miss out on evening activities. However, there's no rule against mini-celebrations or outings during the day. A morning movie or an afternoon BBQ can be just as fun.

3. **Weekend Plans**: If your schedule permits, try to have at least one ordinary day off with your spouse, children, or friends to enjoy activities everyone enjoys.

## Flexibility and Adaptability

1. **Ad Hoc Socializing**: While planning is essential, be open to impromptu social interactions. A spontaneous coffee date or an unplanned quick catch-up call can be invigorating.

2. **Virtual Socializing**: Utilize technology to maintain relationships. Video calls, online games, or even watching a movie together virtually can be great ways to stay connected.

## Maintain Individual Relationships

1. **One-on-One Time**: Individual relationships often take a hit when juggling many commitments. Make sure to spend one-on-one time with your spouse, each child, or close friends to maintain the quality of each relationship.

2. **Surprise Gestures**: A surprise note, a small gift, or even doing a chore for your loved one can go a long way in maintaining the emotional bond, especially when your physical presence is limited.

## Seek Support

1. **Support Groups**: Online communities and support groups exist for people working non-traditional hours. These platforms can offer valuable advice on how others maintain their social and family lives.

2. **Spousal Support**: It's a team effort, especially in a family setting. A supportive spouse can make a difference in how smoothly things run at home, making it easier for you to manage work and personal commitments.

Remember, every relationship requires effort, but the challenges posed by night shift work can be managed with proper planning, open communication, and creativity. While you may have to adapt and compromise, a fulfilling family and social life is possible.

# Financial Planning for Night Shift Nurses

Financial planning is an essential aspect of life that impacts your present and future well-being. When working night shifts, some unique circumstances, such as differential pay and non-traditional hours, can influence your financial landscape. This chapter offers tips on navigating financial planning while considering the particulars of night-shift nursing.

## Differential Pay and Budgeting

1. **Maximize Your Differential**: Night-shift nurses often receive higher hourly rates due to differential pay. Make the most of this by setting aside the extra income for savings,

investments, or paying off debt.

2. **Budget Accordingly**: Since you're earning more, raising your standard of living might be tempting. However, a wise financial move would be to budget as if making a day shift salary and using the extra for specific financial goals.

3. **Emergency Fund**: Your differential pay can be an excellent source for building an emergency fund, a financial cushion that can help you handle unexpected expenses without going into debt.

## Planning and Timing

1. **Off-Peak Benefits**: Take advantage of off-peak hours for grocery shopping or appointments that could save money. Some services may offer discounts during non-peak hours.

2. **Schedule Considerations**: Working non-traditional hours might make consulting with financial advisors who operate during regular business hours challenging. Look for advisors willing to accommodate your schedule.

3. **Online Tools**: Use budgeting and financial tracking tools to manage your finances anytime, suitable for night shift schedules.

## Investments and Retirement

1. **Retirement Funds**: Take advantage of employer-based re-

tirement options like 401(k) plans in the U.S. or RRSPs in Canada. Often, employers will match your contributions up to a certain amount.

2. **Tax Planning**: Consider hiring a tax consultant to help you understand how your additional income from differential pay affects your tax bracket and what deductions you might be eligible for.

3. **Invest Wisely**: Your extra earnings can be a good investment opportunity. Choose investments that align with your financial goals and risk tolerance, whether it's stock, bonds, or real estate.

### Financial Education

1. **Stay Informed**: Financial literacy is crucial for anyone, but night shift nurses should be particularly aware of the unique financial opportunities and challenges they face. Read books, attend seminars, or take online courses to stay informed.

2. **Professional Advice**: Given the complexities of financial planning, professional advice can be invaluable. Whether it's investment strategies, tax planning, or retirement options, consult professionals for a tailored financial plan.

### Long-Term Goals

1. **Home Ownership**: If buying a home is a long-term goal,

your differential pay can contribute significantly to a down payment, allowing you to reach this milestone sooner.

2. **Children's Education**: If you have or plan to have children, consider setting up education savings accounts. Your additional income can help secure an excellent educational foundation for them.

3. **Financial Independence**: By judiciously managing your extra income, achieving financial independence or early retirement becomes a more attainable goal.

Working the night shift can bring about financial opportunities that aren't available to day shift workers. By managing your resources wisely and planning, you can utilize the benefits of night shift work to secure a stable financial future.

# Creating a Restful Environment

## Optimizing Sleep and Relaxation During Daylight Hours

For night shift workers, creating a restful environment during the daylight hours is essential for achieving high-quality sleep and maintaining both physical and mental well-being. While sleeping when the sun is up, and the rest of the world is awake presents unique challenges, there are practical ways to optimize your home environment to ensure you get the rest you need. Here are some tips to help you turn your home into a sanctuary of relaxation and rejuvenation.

## Light Control

1. **Blackout Curtains**: Invest in high-quality blackout curtains to block out natural daylight, allowing your brain to signal to your body that it's time to wind down.

2. **Eye Masks**: As an additional measure, consider wearing an eye mask to block any stray light that may seep in around the curtains.

3. **Soft Lighting**: If you need to get up during your sleep time, use mild or dim lighting to minimize disruption to your sleep cycle.

## Sound Control

1. **White Noise Machine**: Ambient noise can be a significant distraction, especially during the day. A white noise machine can drown out disruptive noises, helping you sleep deeply.

2. **Ear Plugs**: High-quality earplugs can block out external noise, offering a simple, cost-effective solution.

3. **Soundproofing**: If you want to invest more, consider adding soundproofing measures to your room, like acoustic panels or foam.

## Temperature Control

1. **Cool Room**: A cooler room promotes better sleep. Use fans, an air conditioner, or a smart thermostat to maintain a comfortable room temperature.

2. **Breathable Sheets**: Choose light, breathable fabrics like cotton for your bedding to help regulate body temperature during sleep.

## Sleep Accessories

1. **Quality Mattress and Pillows**: Your mattress and pillows significantly affect sleep quality. Opt for materials that offer good support and comfort tailored to your sleep position.
2. **Sleep-Inducing Scents**: Aromatherapy can aid relaxation. Consider a lavender or chamomile diffuser for calming effects.

## Pre-Sleep Rituals

1. **Unplug**: Turn off or silence electronic devices that may emit disruptive sounds or lights. The blue light from screens can interfere with the production of the sleep hormone melatonin.
2. **Relaxation Techniques**: Before bed, engage in relaxation techniques such as deep breathing, gentle stretching, or reading to signal to your body that it's time to wind down.

## Creating a Dedicated Sleep Space

1. **Remove Clutter**: To create a mentally calming environment, keep your sleep space clean and free of clutter.

2. **Designated Sleep Zone**: If possible, use your bedroom only for sleep to create a strong mental association between the space and rest.

3. **Personal Touch**: Add personal touches like photographs or artwork that bring you joy and peace, but avoid overly stimulating or distracting items.

By carefully curating your home environment to support sleep and relaxation, you can significantly improve the quality of your rest. This, in turn, will better equip you to face the unique challenges of working the night shift, supporting both your professional performance and your overall well-being.

# Navigating the Healthcare System

## Leveraging Job Benefits for Optimal Well-being

As a night shift worker in the healthcare industry, you know the toll such a schedule can take on your overall health and well-being. But are you taking full advantage of the range of benefits your job offers to mitigate these effects? From health insurance plans to wellness programs, here are insights into maximizing your employment benefits to support your health and lifestyle.

## Understanding Health Insurance

1. **Choose Wisely**: During open enrollment, take the time to compare different health plans. Consider your current medical needs and potential future issues, especially those that

night shift workers are particularly susceptible to, like sleep disorders.

2. **Know Your Coverage**: Understand what your insurance covers. This includes preventive care services, emergency room visits, specialist consultations, and medications. Take advantage of services that are fully covered whenever possible.

3. **Flexible Spending Accounts (FSAs) or Health Savings Accounts (HSAs)**: If these options are available, consider contributing. They allow you to set aside pre-tax dollars for medical expenses, offering a financial cushion for unexpected health issues.

## Utilizing Wellness Programs

1. **Fitness and Exercise**: Many healthcare employers offer subsidized gym memberships or onsite fitness centers. Exercise is a great way to counterbalance the physical stress of night shift work.

2. **Nutritional Counseling**: Take advantage of any nutritional programs your employer may offer. Proper nutrition is crucial when your biological clock is out of sync with your work schedule.

3. **Mental Health Support**: Stress management and mental well-being are vital for night shift workers. Some employers offer free or discounted mental health services, like counselling or mindfulness and stress reduction workshops.

## Telehealth Services

1. **Convenience**: Because of your non-traditional working hours, scheduling healthcare appointments can be challenging. Telehealth services offer a flexible alternative, allowing you to consult healthcare providers at times convenient.

2. **Range of Services**: Many telehealth platforms offer primary care consultations, mental health support, and specialist visits. Check whether your health insurance covers telehealth services and to what extent.

## Onsite Healthcare Services

1. **Checkups and Screenings**: Some extensive healthcare facilities offer onsite services like health checkups, flu shots, and biometric screenings. Utilize these whenever possible to keep track of your health metrics.

2. **Employee Assistance Programs (EAPs)**: These programs often offer services from legal advice to mental health support. If you're facing difficulties, this is a confidential and usually free way to seek help.

## Continued Education and Skill Enhancement

1. **Skill Development**: Many employers offer seminars, workshops, or even tuition reimbursement for healthcare-related

courses. These opportunities are not just career-boosting but can also improve your knowledge and competence, adding to your well-being at work.

2. **Certifications**: Maintaining and gaining additional certifications can make you more valuable in your role and often come with the added benefit of boosting your self-esteem and job satisfaction.

Navigating the healthcare system and understanding your benefits can sometimes be daunting. However, taking the time to delve into these options can significantly benefit your physical and mental well-being. As a night shift worker, making informed choices about your healthcare options is an empowering step toward a more balanced and fulfilling life.

# Safety Measures

## Staying Alert and Reducing Errors During Night Shifts

Working the night shift, particularly in a healthcare setting, presents medical and general challenges that demand heightened attention to safety. From ensuring precise medication administration to avoiding physical accidents, the margin for error is slim. Here are some guidelines to help you stay alert focused and maintain the highest safety standards during your night shifts.

### Medical Safety Measures

1. **Double-Check Medications**: Always double or even triple-check medications, dosages, and patient information, especially during the handoff from one shift to another. Fatigue can lead to errors, so taking extra precautions is vital.

2. **Regular Monitoring**: Patients' vital signs and conditions must be consistently monitored, even more so at night when staffing may be reduced and patients are less likely to be alert.

3. **Use Alarms and Reminders**: Take advantage of alarm features on medical devices and set manual reminders to regularly check high-risk patients' medication times or complete critical tasks.

4. **Follow Sterile Techniques**: Rigorously adhere to sterilization protocols for instruments and your hygiene to minimize infection risks.

5. **Protocol Awareness**: Ensure you're up-to-date with the latest healthcare protocols and emergency procedures. Regularly reviewing these can make a significant difference in a critical situation.

## General Safety Measures

1. **Stay Hydrated and Nourished**: Dehydration and low blood sugar can impair your cognitive functions and attention span, putting you at higher risk for errors.

2. **Scheduled Breaks**: Take short, regular breaks to stand, stretch, and walk a little. This helps to reset your focus and alleviate physical and mental fatigue.

3. **Manage Caffeine Intake**: While caffeine can temporarily boost, excessive amounts can lead to jitteriness, decreased focus, and a crash later on. Aim to consume it strategically

rather than continuously.

4. **Situational Awareness**: Always be aware of your surroundings. This involves knowing the locations of emergency exits, fire extinguishers, and other safety equipment and being alert to any unusual activities or potential hazards in your environment.

## Tools for Alertness

1. **Ergonomic Workspaces**: Where possible, ensure your workspace is ergonomically designed to minimize physical strain. This can help maintain higher levels of alertness.

2. **Alertness Apps**: Various mobile apps are designed to help healthcare workers stay alert by offering periodic reminders, focus-enhancing games, or even short physical exercises.

3. **Collaborative Vigilance**: Work as a team to stay alert. Check-in with coworkers to ensure that everyone stays focused, and don't hesitate to seek help if you're feeling exhausted.

## Communication

1. **Handoff Briefings**: Whether handing off your responsibilities to someone else or taking over for another shift, thorough and accurate communication is crucial for maintaining patient safety.

2. **Report Incidents**: Any incidents, even minor ones, should be immediately reported and adequately documented. This helps identify patterns and improvement areas, thereby enhancing overall safety.

## Personal Safety

1. **Safe Commute**: Your safety measures shouldn't end when your shift does. Ensure you're fit to drive home or arrange for transportation if you're too tired.

2. **Security Measures**: Be aware of and adhere to your facility's security protocols, such as always wearing identification and ensuring that all restricted areas are kept secure.

The night shift poses unique challenges that require a vigilant approach to safety. By following these guidelines, you're not just safeguarding yourself but also significantly contributing to the well-being and security of your patients and colleagues. A proactive stance on safety is the best defence against the heightened risks associated with night shift work.

# Legal Rights and Responsibilities

## Labor Laws and Regulations Affecting Night Shift Workers in Canada and the United States

Both Canada and the United States have established labor laws and regulations that impact night shift workers. These legal frameworks help protect workers from exploitation, ensure fair compensation, and mandate rest periods. Here is an overview of some key laws and how they affect night shift workers in these countries:

### Overtime Pay

1. **United States - Fair Labor Standards Act (FLSA)**: Under the FLSA, non-exempt employees in the United States are

generally entitled to receive "time-and-a-half" pay for any hours worked beyond 40 hours in a single workweek.

2. **Canada - Provincial Labor Standards**: Overtime laws can vary by province in Canada, but generally, employees are entitled to 1.5 times their regular wage for any hours worked beyond the standard work week, which can vary from 40 to 44 hours depending on the province.

### Mandatory Breaks

1. **United States**: Break laws also vary by state, but under the FLSA, short breaks of 20 minutes or less are generally considered compensable time, whereas meal breaks of 30 minutes or more are not.

2. **Canada**: In Canada, break laws are regulated by provincial labor codes. Generally, employees are entitled to a 30-minute meal break after five hours of continuous work.

### Shift Differential

1. **United States**: While not federally mandated, many employers in the United States offer a shift differential, or premium pay, for employees who work night shifts.

2. **Canada**: Similar to the U.S., shift differential is often provided in Canada, although it is not mandated by law. The specifics may be outlined in employment contracts or collective bargaining agreements.

## Rest Periods Between Shifts

1. **United States**: There is generally no federal requirement for the amount of time that must pass between shifts, but some states have specific "day of rest" laws.

2. **Canada**: Canadian labor laws may mandate a minimum number of hours that must elapse between shifts, and these can vary by province.

## Safety Standards

1. **United States - Occupational Safety and Health Act (OSHA)**: Employers are required to provide a safe working environment, and this extends to night shift workers as well.

2. **Canada - Canadian Centre for Occupational Health and Safety (CCOHS)**: Similarly, Canadian employers are obliged to ensure that all employees, including night shift workers, are provided a safe working environment.

## Family and Medical Leave

1. **United States - Family and Medical Leave Act (FMLA)**: Eligible employees can take up to 12 weeks of unpaid, job-protected leave for specified family and medical reasons.

2. **Canada - Employment Insurance (EI)**: Canada provides various types of leave through its Employment Insurance

system, including maternity, parental, and caregiving benefits.

## Union and Collective Bargaining

1. **United States and Canada**: In both countries, night shift workers have the right to join or form a union and engage in collective bargaining, which can often result in better pay and working conditions.

## Final Thoughts

Understanding your legal rights and responsibilities is crucial for protecting yourself as a night shift worker. If you have specific concerns or questions, consider consulting a labor law attorney or your union representative for advice tailored to your situation. Always read your employment contract carefully and be aware of any state or provincial laws that may offer additional protections or benefits.

# The Power of Teamwork

## Fostering a Positive Work Environment Among Night Shift Colleagues

The night shift can often feel like an isolating experience, with the hospital or facility quieter than during the day and fewer staff on hand. This solitude can make teamwork all the more critical, not just for the practical completion of tasks but also for boosting morale and job satisfaction among night shift workers. Fostering a positive work environment starts with every team member and goes beyond simply completing tasks efficiently. Here are some strategies to build a cohesive, engaged, and happy night shift team:

### Open Communication

1. **Regular Briefings**: Start or end your shifts with team briefings to discuss what has happened, what needs to happen, and any concerns or suggestions team members might have.

2. **Honest Feedback**: Encourage an environment where constructive criticism is welcomed. I am open about what can be improved, which leads to a more efficient and content team.

3. **Active Listening**: The best communicators are also excellent listeners. Make sure everyone feels heard and acknowledged.

## Mutual Respect

1. **Shared Responsibility**: Make sure that tasks are evenly distributed among team members so no one feels overwhelmed or underutilized.

2. **Acknowledge Expertise**: Everyone has different strengths and skills. Recognize and utilize the unique talents each person brings to the team.

## Team-building Activities

1. **Brief Team Games**: Short and fun team-building games can invigorate a team and improve social bonds.

2. **Celebrations**: Birthdays, anniversaries, or achieving team targets—no milestone is too small to acknowledge and celebrate.

## Psychological Safety

1. **Zero Tolerance for Bullying**: Make it known that harassment or bullying will not be tolerated and ensure there are confidential avenues for reporting such issues.

2. **Encourage Open Dialogue**: Team members should feel safe sharing their concerns or ideas without fear of ridicule or retribution.

## Professional Development

1. **Skill Sharing**: Encourage team members to teach each other something new. It could be a job-related skill or even a fun activity like making origami.

2. **Mentoring**: More experienced team members can advise newer or less professional staff. This can be formalized through a mentoring program or happen more informally.

## Health and Well-being

1. **Work-life Balance**: Be respectful of each other's time. Don't expect team members to routinely stay late or skip breaks, which can lead to burnout.

2. **Self-care Reminder**: Remind each other about the importance of taking short breaks, eating well, and staying hydrated. Sometimes, in the hustle of the night shift, these essential

practices can be forgotten.

## Foster Inclusion

1. **Celebrate Diversity**: A diverse workforce brings a range of experiences and viewpoints. Celebrate this diversity and make everyone feel included and valued.
2. **Inclusive Language**: Use language that makes all team members feel included, regardless of their background, and encourage others to do the same.

## Final Thoughts

Building a strong and cohesive night shift team doesn't happen overnight, but the benefits are worth the effort. A supportive group can significantly improve the experience of working night shifts, making it more manageable and enjoyable. After all, we're all in this together, and the night shift becomes much brighter when you know you can rely on a great team.

# Parenthood and the Night Shift

## Tips for Managing Family Responsibilities

Juggling the responsibilities of parenthood with the unique challenges of night shift work can often feel like walking a tightrope. Not only do you have to maintain your performance at work, but you also need to ensure that your family life doesn't take a backseat. The non-traditional hours can complicate childcare arrangements, disrupt family routines, and make attending important events and milestones difficult. Here are some strategies to help you balance family commitments with your night shift schedule.

## Childcare Solutions

1. **Shift Swapping**: If your workplace allows it, consider

swapping shifts with coworkers to be available for important family events or appointments.

2. **Extended Family and Friends**: Sometimes, relatives and close friends can be a lifesaver regarding last-minute or short-term childcare needs.
3. **Childcare Services**: Some areas have childcare services that cater to parents working non-traditional hours—research options in your community.
4. **In-home Care**: Depending on your circumstances, hiring a nanny or babysitter to look after your children during your night shifts may be feasible.

## Family Scheduling

1. **Shared Calendar**: Use a shared digital calendar to keep track of work schedules, school events, doctor's appointments, and other important dates so that all family members are in the loop.
2. **Meal Prepping**: Prepare meals ahead of time or consider batch cooking to ensure that your family has nutritious meals ready, even when you're not there to cook.
3. **Chore Charts**: Assign age-appropriate chores to children and other family members to distribute household responsibilities more evenly.

## Quality Time

1. **Morning Routine**: If you return home when your children are getting ready for school, make that your time to have breakfast together or help them prepare for their day.

2. **Weekend Plans**: Maximize your days off by planning special activities or outings with the family. Quality time is more about how you spend it than how much time you have.

3. **Virtual Check-ins**: If you can take short breaks during your shift, a quick video call can connect you with your family.

## Emotional Support

1. **Open Communication**: Keep the lines of communication open with your partner and children. Make sure they understand the reasons for your work schedule and discuss any feelings or concerns they may have.

2. **Support Network**: Utilize online forums, local parenting groups, or other community resources to connect with other parents in similar situations for advice and emotional support.

## Flexibility and Back-Up Plans

1. **Emergency Contacts**: Always have a list of reliable emergency contacts who can step in when unexpected work situations arise.

2. **Flex Time**: If your employer offers flexible work arrangements, use this to your advantage to align your schedule as closely as possible with your family's needs.

## Prioritizing Self-Care

1. **Rest**: Ensuring you get enough rest is vital for your performance at work and your ability to be present and engaged during family time.

2. **Exercise and Nutrition**: Taking care of yourself physically can boost your energy levels and overall well-being, making it easier to manage the demands of work and family life.

Balancing parenthood and night shift work is no small feat, but it's not impossible. With some planning, open communication, and a support network, you can fulfill your duties at work and home. While it may require sacrifices and adjustments, remember that this is a phase, and conditions will change. The most important thing is staying committed to finding that balance for your career and family.

# Career Development

## Managing Growth and Skill Development on the Night Shift

Working the night shift has unique challenges but should not impede your career growth and skill development. If you are committed to advancing professionally while working non-traditional hours, there are strategies and best practices that can help you achieve your career goals. Below are some tips for managing your career development effectively while on the night shift.

### Skill Enhancement

1. **Online Courses**: One of the advantages of working the

night shift is the potential for quieter periods. Utilize this time effectively by enrolling in online courses that boost your professional skills.

2. **Certifications**: Many professions offer certificates that can make you more marketable. Find opportunities to attain these through online programs or workshops that fit your schedule.

3. **Job Rotation**: If possible, rotate through different roles or departments to gain a well-rounded skill set. This will not only make your job more exciting but also make you more versatile and valuable to your organization.

## Networking

1. **Social Media and Online Forums**: Use professional networking sites like LinkedIn to connect with colleagues and professionals in your field. Participate in relevant online forums to stay updated and visible in your professional community.

2. **Industry Events**: Though many events may be scheduled during your sleep hours, attend relevant seminars, webinars, or workshops when you can. You could also catch up on missed events through recorded sessions.

3. **Internal Networking**: Use any overlapping time between the day and night shifts to network with colleagues and superiors who work different hours. Keep the channels of communication open with daytime management to stay in

the loop.

## Mentorship and Guidance

1. **Find a Mentor**: A mentor can provide invaluable insights into career growth and personal development. Find someone whose career path you admire, and approach them for mentorship.

2. **Peer Support**: Share experiences and tips with colleagues interested in career development. You could even create an informal "career growth" group to share resources and encouragement.

## Performance Reviews and Advancement

1. **Regular Feedback**: Given the different schedules, it's crucial to maintain normal channels for performance evaluations. Request supervisor feedback and offer insights during assessments to keep track of your career goals.

2. **Show Initiative**: Even on the night shift, opportunities will arise for you to demonstrate leadership or specialized skills. Seize these opportunities to show you're ready for more responsibility.

## Work-Life Balance

1. **Time Management**: Effective time management is crucial

when balancing work, skill development, and personal life. Create a realistic schedule with time for self-study, relaxation, and family.

2. **Setting Boundaries**: Be sure to set clear boundaries to prevent burnout. Your career is a marathon, not a sprint.

## Personal Branding

1. **Showcase Achievements**: Record your achievements, completed courses, and any kudos you receive from colleagues or supervisors. These can be useful for performance reviews or future job applications.
2. **Professional Portfolio**: Depending on your field, maintain an updated portfolio of your work. This can be useful for internal reviews or external job opportunities.

By taking a proactive approach to your career development, the night shift doesn't have to hinder your professional growth. Instead, with careful planning, it can be a unique opportunity to demonstrate your skills, initiative, and dedication to your career.

# Burnout and Coping Mechanisms

## Navigating the Unique Challenges of Night Shift Work

Burnout is pervasive in many professions, but the unique demands of night shift work can exacerbate stress and fatigue, making you more susceptible. Burnout manifests physically and emotionally, impacting your job performance, relationships, and overall well-being. Recognizing the signs specific to night shift work and employing coping mechanisms can help you mitigate its impact and maintain a healthier work-life balance.

## Signs of Burnout Specific to Night Shift Work

1. **Chronic Fatigue**: While it's common to feel tired when adjusting to night shift work, ongoing, debilitating fatigue is a red flag.

2. **Social Isolation**: Working when most people are off-duty can lead to feelings of loneliness and disconnect, contributing to burnout.

3. **Increased Irritability**: A disrupted circadian rhythm can affect your mood. Take note if you become more irritable at work or home.

4. **Cognitive Decline**: Difficulty focusing, memory issues, and declining problem-solving abilities can all indicate burnout.

5. **Physical Ailments**: Frequent headaches, gastrointestinal issues, and increased susceptibility to illness can result from prolonged stress and inadequate rest.

6. **Decreased Job Satisfaction**: A lack of enthusiasm for your job, especially if you once enjoyed it, is a hallmark sign of burnout.

7. **Neglecting Self-Care**: An obvious but often overlooked sign is neglecting personal well-being, including inadequate nutrition, exercise, and sleep.

## Coping Strategies to Mitigate Burnout

1. **Self-Assessment**: Regularly take stock of your emotional and physical well-being. Being honest with yourself is the first step in addressing burnout.

2. **Consult a Professional**: If you identify signs of burnout, consult healthcare professionals for medical and psychological support.

3. **Set Boundaries**: Limit the number of extra shifts or overtime you agree to, and don't be afraid to say no when you're reaching your limit.

4. **Quality Rest**: Prioritize quality sleep by creating a sleep-conducive environment and sticking to a sleep schedule, even on your days off.

5. **Physical Activity**: Incorporate regular exercise into your routine. Physical activity is proven to reduce stress and improve mental well-being.

6. **Social Support**: Maintain a strong support network by scheduling time with friends and family and staying connected digitally when face-to-face interactions are impossible.

7. **Nutrition**: Eating a balanced diet rich in nutrients can significantly affect your energy levels and resilience to stress. Avoid excessive caffeine and sugar, which can lead to energy crashes.

8. **Mindfulness and Relaxation**: Techniques such as mindfulness, meditation, and deep-breathing exercises can effectively reduce stress.

9. **Professional Development**: Feeling stagnant can contribute to burnout. Actively seek career growth and skill development opportunities to keep your job engaging.

10. **Take Time Off**: Use your vacation days, and don't feel guilty about it. Time away from work can provide much-needed physical and mental restoration.

11. **Change of Scenery**: Sometimes, a temporary shift change or even a different job role can provide a new perspective and alleviate feelings of burnout.

Recognizing and addressing burnout specific to night shift work is crucial for your long-term well-being and career satisfaction. Actively mitigating stress and maintaining a healthy work-life balance can rejuvenate your enthusiasm for your job and improve your overall quality of life.

# Case Studies

## Thriving in the Night Shift Lifestyle as a Nurse

Adapting to the night shift lifestyle in nursing is no small feat, but many have navigated this path successfully, finding ways to balance work, personal life, and health. Below are case studies of nurses who have turned the challenges of night shift work into opportunities for growth and fulfillment.

## Case Study 1: Emily - Balancing Family Life

Emily, a mother of two young children, chose night shift work to coordinate childcare with her husband, who works during the day. She maximizes her differential pay by funnelling it into a college savings account for her children.

**Key Takeaways:**

- Effective communication and planning with family.

- Utilizing extra pay for long-term family goals.

### Case Study 2: David - Career Advancement

David is a night shift nurse who used the relative quiet of the late hours to further his education. While juggling work and study was tough, he completed an advanced nursing degree, which led to a promotion.

**Key Takeaways**:

- I am using downtime effectively for career advancement.
- We are prioritizing long-term goals over short-term comforts.

### Case Study 3: Aisha - Health and Well-being

Aisha faced initial health setbacks when she started night shifts, including weight gain and disrupted sleep. However, she overcame these challenges by embracing a strict diet and exercise regimen, eventually running a half-marathon.

**Key Takeaways**:

- Commitment to physical health can yield remarkable results.
- An initial setback is not a final verdict; adaptive strategies can work.

### Case Study 4: Carlos - Social Life and Networking

Carlos, who loves socializing, initially found night shifts isolating. However, he set up a book club among night shift colleagues and kept in touch with friends through video calls during break times, maintaining a healthy social life.

**Key Takeaways**:

- Creativity in maintaining social connections.
- Fostering a community among night shift colleagues can provide social support.

## Case Study 5: Brenda - Financial Security

After years of living paycheck to paycheck, Brenda decided to take control of her finances. She hired a financial advisor willing to work with her night shift schedule and invested her differential pay wisely, achieving financial independence in just six years.

**Key Takeaways**:

- Financial planning is possible and beneficial, even with a demanding schedule.
- Professional advice can be tailored to suit unconventional working hours.

## Case Study 6: Tom - Mental Health Advocacy

Tom used his experience as a night shift nurse to become an advocate for mental health in the workplace. Recognizing the unique stressors, he worked with management to provide mental health resources for night shift staff.

**Key Takeaways**:

- Identifying a problem can be the first step to creating systemic change.

- Advocacy can result in tangible benefits for the broader community.

### Case Study 7: Sophia - Combining Passions

Sophia is a registered nurse who is also a passionate writer. She found that the calm of the night shift allowed her mental space to think creatively. She started jotting down her thoughts and ideas during her breaks, eventually publishing a collection of short stories inspired by the resilience she witnessed in her patients.

**Key Takeaways**:

- Finding time for personal passions can enrich your career.
- Night shifts can provide the quiet needed for introspective or creative tasks.

### Case Study 8: Raj - Entrepreneurial Spirit

Raj had always been interested in healthcare technology. Working night shifts gave him the flexibility to start a small business focused on developing healthcare apps designed for nurses. He managed to attend meetings and network during the day, taking naps before his night shifts.

**Key Takeaways**:

- Night shift work can offer flexibility for other entrepreneurial pursuits.
- Efficient time management can allow you to juggle multiple

commitments successfully.

### Case Study 9: Lisa - Educational Mentorship

Lisa took the initiative to create an informal educational program for her night shift colleagues, focusing on continual learning and skill development. This made her a valuable asset to her team and improved morale, making night shifts more engaging and intellectually fulfilling for everyone involved.

**Key Takeaways**:

- Leadership opportunities exist in all settings, even during night shifts.
- Enhancing the team's skillset benefits individual members and the organization.

### Case Study 10: Alex - Environmental Impact

Concerned about the waste produced in healthcare settings, Alex used the quieter moments of the night shift to research and implement a recycling program tailored for his department. His initiative not only reduced waste but also caught the attention of the hospital's administration, leading to hospital-wide adoption of more sustainable practices.

**Key Takeaways**:

- Night shifts can offer time to focus on broader issues affecting your workplace.
- Small changes can lead to significant, wide-reaching im-

provements.

Each of these added case studies highlights the diverse ways night shift nurses can leverage their unique work schedules for personal development, social good, and professional growth. Whether you're interested in financial planning, continuing education, or even launching a side business, the examples of these resilient individuals prove that with some ingenuity and a lot of dedication, the night shift doesn't have to be a career or lifestyle hindrance; it can be an opportunity.

# Frequently Asked Questions

## Common Questions and Misconceptions About Night Shift Work in Nursing

Working the night shift in nursing presents its own unique set of challenges and opportunities. Given its non-traditional hours, it's often the subject of numerous questions and misconceptions. Here, we address some of the most commonly asked questions to shed light on what it's like to work the night shift as a nurse.

### Q: Is night shift nursing less busy than day shifts?

**A:** While night shifts can have periods of lower activity, they are not universally "less busy." Patient needs can arise at any hour, and staffing is often reduced at night, which means that night-shift nurses may need to manage a broad range of responsibilities.

### Q: Do night shift nurses get paid more?

**A:** In most healthcare settings in the U.S. and Canada, night shift nurses typically receive a differential pay rate to compensate for the unconventional hours. However, the amount can vary by institution and geographic location.

### Q: Is working the night shift indeed terrible for your health?

**A:** While there are challenges associated with night shift work, such as disruptions to your circadian rhythm, it doesn't have to be detrimental to your health if appropriately managed. Adhering to a consistent sleep schedule, maintaining a balanced diet, and incorporating regular exercise can mitigate many health risks.

### Q: Can working night shifts negatively affect your social and family life?

**A:** While night shifts can make socializing and family commitments more challenging, many people successfully balance work, family, and social lives by setting priorities and effectively using their time off.

### Q: Is getting a job as a night shift nurse easier?

**A:** Often, night shift positions are easier to come by than day shift roles, especially for newly graduated nurses, due to lower competition.

However, "easier" doesn't mean "easy," and all nursing roles require high skill and commitment.

### Q: Do night shift nurses handle fewer procedures than day shift nurses?

**A:** While specific procedures and administrative tasks may be scheduled during daytime hours, night shift nurses are fully trained and capable of handling various clinical systems, as patient needs can arise anytime.

### Q: Can you quickly switch from the night shift to the day shift?

**A:** The ease of switching shifts often depends on institutional policies, staffing needs, and seniority. Some workplaces have a rotating schedule, while others require a formal process to change from night to day shifts.

### Q: Is working night shifts a career disadvantage?

**A:** Not necessarily. Many nurses have built successful careers while working the night shift. It can even be advantageous for those looking to gain more experience quickly, take on additional responsibilities, or pursue further education.

### Q: Is it true that only junior nurses work night shifts?

**A:** No, nurses of all experience levels work night shifts for various reasons, including personal preference, family needs, or professional development opportunities.

## Q: Do you have to work night shifts as a nurse?

**A:** While many nurses will experience night shift work at some point in their careers, especially as new grads, it is not a universal requirement. Nursing career paths are incredibly diverse, and many roles involve only day shift work.

By understanding the realities of night shift nursing, you can make informed decisions about your career path and how to manage the challenges and opportunities it offers effectively.

# Resources

1. **"Why We Sleep" by Matthew Walker**: A deep dive into sleep science, helping you understand its importance.
2. **"Eat Sleep Work Repeat" by Bruce Daisley**: Tips on balancing your work life, which is especially relevant for night shift nurses.
3. **"The Power of Habit" by Charles Duhigg**: Learn how to form and maintain habits crucial for adapting to a night shift schedule.
4. **"Burnout: The Secret to Unlocking the Stress Cycle" by Emily Nagoski and Amelia Nagoski**:

## Websites

1. **RegisteredNurseRN.com**
2. **Nurse.org**
3. **SleepFoundation.org**
4. **Healthline**

Printed in Great Britain
by Amazon

34072124R00040